SPIRITUAL POWER

HOW TO GET IT
HOW TO GIVE IT

SPIRITUAL POWER

HOW TO GET IT
HOW TO GIVE IT

*The authoritative guide to the
baptism in the Holy Spirit with the
evidence of speaking in tongues*

By Don W. Basham

KIDWELL
PUBLISHING

Spiritual Power
Reprint Edition
(Originally published by Whitaker House under the
title, *Ministering the Baptism of the Holy Spirit*, which was
subsequently revised and titled, *Spiritual Power*)

ISBN: 978-0-9817634-8-4
Printed in the United States of America

Reprint published by Kidwell Publishing
www.kidwellpublishing.com

Cover design by Tom Cunningham
www.advanced-advertising.com

Table of Contents

Introduction

A few years ago, the author of this book was the speaker at the monthly Full Gospel Business Men's Fellowship chapter meeting in Greensburg, Pennsylvania, near Pittsburgh. The Greensburg FGBMFI chapter is a strong chapter and well-attended. On that March night there were nearly 700 people present.

Don Basham began his message with some personal testimony. But in a matter of minutes, the Holy Spirit led him into presenting almost word for word the message this book contains. Although he spoke primarily to those who had already received the baptism to encourage them in ministering to others, nevertheless, at the end of the meeting, an invitation was given for any who might be seeking the baptism in the Holy Spirit to retire to an adjoining room for prayer.

The simplicity of the teaching, combined with the confidence with which Don Basham spoke, had created an expectancy on the part of the people which enabled the Holy Spirit to move with great effectiveness and power. The response to the invitation was overwhelming, and the prayer room quickly filled with people. There they heard the simple instructions contained in chapter five of this book. Then, when prayer was offered, it was like the day of Pentecost all over again. Almost immediately, over 100 people received the baptism in the Holy Spirit and began praising God in other tongues.

We believe the publication of the basic message presented that night will also be mightily used of God to further the twentieth century Pentecost of which we are a part.

Robert E. Whitaker, President

Whitaker House

Chapter 1

Ministering the Baptism in the Holy Spirit

If you are truly a Christian, it is an exciting time to be alive! God is pouring out His Holy Spirit and the Church of Jesus Christ is in the midst of world-wide revival.

Christianity has known great revivals before, under men like Martin Luther, John Calvin, John Wesley and Dwight L. Moody. But the revival we are experiencing today is not the same as those of the past. The great revivals of history were characterized by two central features—they were confined to a particular country, such as Germany, England, Scotland, or the American frontier, and they revolved around some particular spiritual leader or group of leaders. But those two features are missing today, for today's revival is not restricted to any single country or continent and it knows no single spiritual leader. Many of us believe it is the beginning of the last great revival, the one destined to usher in the return of Jesus Christ and the end of the age—the revival prophesied by Joel and quoted by Peter on the Day of Pentecost.

> And it shall come to pass *in the last days* saith God, I will pour out of my Spirit upon all flesh—and your young men shall see visions and your old men shall dream dreams, and on my servants and my handmaidens I will pour out in those days of my Spirit and they shall prophesy.
>
> —Acts 2:17-18

Central to this great revival is the experience known as the baptism in the Holy Spirit. Literally millions of Christians have moved into this spiritual empowering in the last few decades and millions more are interested in it. Many of you who read this little book have already experienced baptism in the Holy Spirit. And you may have already discovered that it is one thing to have the experience and quite another thing to be able to teach, interpret or minister it to others.

For a number of years I wrestled personally with this very difficulty. I knew what had happened to me and could testify to it, but had real difficulty in teaching or explaining it to those who raised questions about it which I could not answer, especially those who had a broader general grasp of Scripture than I had. I often came away saddened and frustrated. I felt like the blind man whom Jesus healed. When criticized by the Jewish authorities, he said, "One thing I know, that though I was blind, now I see"(John 9:25). That's the way I felt about trying to share the baptism in the Holy Spirit. All I seemed to be able to say was, "Before I *didn't* have it, but now I *do* have it." It had made a profound difference in my life but I was totally inadequate in sharing it with others.

But time and experience have combined to change that situation. In recent years, I've found myself traveling all over the United States and in a number of foreign countries as well, teaching and ministering the baptism in the Holy Spirit. In the process, I've made many mistakes and learned not a few lessons. In teaching missions, I have regularly been confronted with most of the objections and questions concerning the Baptism in the Holy Spirit and speaking in tongues. Out of those many encounters has come a simple, basic message which has proved helpful, both to those who are seeking the baptism and those who are seeking to minister it. The purpose of this book is to pass that message on.

It is written primarily for the benefit of those who have received the baptism in the Holy Spirit with the evidence of speaking in tongues, and who are now finding increasing opportunity to minister the experience to other Christians. I feel the message is timely since many of our preconceived notions about difficulties in receiving the Holy Spirit are being swept away. Traditionally, it has been thought necessary that those seeking more of God, or seeking the infilling of the Holy Spirit should find some church altar and pray and agonize and "tarry" before God until they either become discouraged and give up, or finally "receive the blessing." And truthfully, we are grateful for the many Christians who agonized their way into a fuller Christian life by this, or whatever means.

But today, God has clearly demonstrated that such periods of agonizing and tarrying are neither scriptural nor necessary. We have discovered that by proper teaching from the Word of God, Christians may be brought to the point where, *by faith*, they can step easily and quickly into the baptism in the Holy Spirit, with all the empowering results which have traditionally followed the experience. According to Scripture, the only people who ever "tarried" to receive the Holy Spirit were the one hundred and twenty who were waiting in the upper room for the coming of the Holy Spirit on the day of Pentecost. Since that day when Jesus sent the Holy Spirit in fulfillment of His promise (Acts 1:4-5), He has been present with us, available and accessible to all who open their hearts and lives to His empowering, and who are longing to receive the spiritual gifts and ministries He brings.

So primarily for those seeking to minister the baptism in the Holy Spirit, but also for any Christian who has not yet received the baptism but may be seeking it, we offer this material which has been shared in hundreds of meetings and seminars where many Christians have subsequently received the baptism in the Holy Spirit with the scriptural evidence of speaking in other tongues.

Chapter 2

The Baptism in the Holy Spirit as a Second Experience

One common objection among Christians concerning the baptism in the Holy Spirit stems from the difficulty of seeing it as a second, separate experience following conversion or rebirth.

"I thought I received the Holy Spirit when I became a Christian," is the way the objection is frequently voiced. Since it is a spiritual law that we receive from God in terms of our asking (Matthew 7:7-8), it must be obvious that if people don't know there is an empowering of God beyond conversion, they won't ask for it. Therefore, the initial task in helping people to receive the baptism in the Holy Spirit is to make it clear to them from the Word of God that there *is* such an experience, and that those who have received Jesus Christ as Savior (John 3:16) may also encounter Him as the one who baptized in the Holy Spirit (Luke 3:16).

Now, concerning the work of the Holy Spirit in the believer's life at the point of conversion: Of course the Holy Spirit is operative in conversion since Paul says, "No one can say Jesus Christ is Lord except by the Holy Spirit." (1 Corinthians 12:3). The Holy Spirit is present in conversion to introduce the unbeliever to Jesus Christ as Savior.

But we are not talking about the *introductory* ministry of the Holy Spirit to the unbeliever— we're speaking of the subsequent *empowering* ministry of the Holy Spirit for the believers. We are speaking of that experience which Jesus promised when He told his disciples (who already knew Him as Savior) "You will receive power when the Holy Spirit has come upon you" (Acts 1:8).

The Scriptures draw a very clear distinction between the two experiences, especially in the book of Acts. Are you aware that the book of Acts is the only book in the entire Bible which contains the record of the life and activities of the first Christians? That it is the only narrative we have of life in the early church? The Gospels are stories of the life of Jesus—the epistles are teaching letters, dealing with problems and difficulties in the Christian life, interpreting and explaining the provisions and promises of God to members of the Body of Christ. But only the book of Acts records the actual life and experience of the church of the New Testament age. And when we examine the book of Acts, we find five passages which describe the outpouring of the Holy Spirit in what we've come to call the baptism in the Holy Spirit. Here's the list of those five passages with a brief description of each incident:

Acts 2:1-21

The Day of Pentecost. The Holy Spirit was poured out on the 120 gathered in the upper room and they all began to speak in other tongues.

Acts 8:4-17

The Samaritan revival under the preaching of Philip. Miracles and signs and wonders accompany Philip's preaching. Peter and John come down from Jerusalem to minister the baptism in the Holy Spirit to the new converts "for as yet He had fallen on none of them."

Acts 9:1-19

The conversion and subsequent healing and baptism in the Holy Spirit of Saul who became Paul. Converted on the road to Damascus, he is healed of his blindness and filled with the Holy Spirit when Ananias comes and prays for him.

Acts 10:34-46

Peter preaches to the household of Cornelius. The people receive forgiveness of sins in the name of Jesus, are converted, and immediately the Holy Spirit falls, and they begin to speak in tongues and magnify God.

Acts 19:1-6

Paul finds twelve disciples at Ephesus who know Jesus as Savior but have not received the baptism in the Holy Spirit. He prays for them and they receive and begin to speak in tongues and prophesy.

From an examination of all five accounts we see the same truth emerging—that conversion is one experience and the baptism in the Holy Spirit is a second, subsequent experience. Now let us examine each of the passages of scripture more in detail.

Acts 2:1-21
PENTECOST

Events prior to the day of Pentecost clearly reveal that one hundred and twenty in the upper room were all believers in Jesus Christ. They were followers of His, they had witnessed His crucifixion and resurrection, they knew He had died for their sins and that He was their Risen Savior. They had heard Him commission them to go into all the world and preach the gospel and had seen Him ascend into heaven.

But knowing Jesus was their Lord and Savior was not enough—at least, not in the mind of the Lord Himself. For He had told them to wait in Jerusalem until they were clothed with power from on high (Luke 24:49).

I must admit that for some years I preached and taught concerning the baptism in the Holy Spirit as if it were a kind of optional or elective course in the school of the Christian life. But no more. I see now it is not an elective, but a *required* course. Required, not for salvation, but for truly victorious Christian living. I see now that all the centuries the church of Jesus Christ has been trying to proclaim the gospel *without* the baptism in the Holy Spirit, she has been doing it in direct disobedience to the clear command of Jesus who, *after* He had commissioned his disciples to go and "teach all nations" (Matthew 28:19-20), nevertheless said "wait" or "tarry" (Luke 24:49). "Don't try to go teach and preach until you have been properly empowered." That's what Jesus was saying.

And that is just what happened on the day of Pentecost—those 120 believers in the upper room were *empowered*, supernaturally, by the Holy Spirit. The miraculous evidence of their empowering was the manifestation of speaking in tongues. And further evidence of the effectiveness of that empowering was that old cowardly Peter, who had denied Jesus three times on the night of the crucifixion and had led the disciples into hiding for fear of Jews after the resurrection, was so transformed that he stood to his feet and preached an anointed message which led to the conversion of three thousand people.

Acts 8:4-17

PHILIP'S REVIVAL IN SAMARIA

The second of the five accounts of the Holy Spirit baptism is found in the eighth chapter of Acts. Philip, one of the first deacons ordained in the church, goes to a Samaritan city, and as he begins to preach the gospel, a great revival breaks out. Miracles accompany the preaching of the Word of God. It is a revival in which "signs and wonders" put the divine stamp of authority and approval on the gospel message. People turn from paganism to Jesus Christ—from sin to salvation, from darkness to light. The new converts are baptized in water in the name of the Lord Jesus, thus becoming full-fledged members of the church, the Body of Christ. They are Christians.

Yet strangely, when word gets back to the apostles at Jerusalem about the Samaritan revival, we find them responding, not in terms of what *is* happening in Samaria but in terms of what *isn't* happening. In the thinking of the apostles there is a vital, missing element in the miracle-working revival Philip has underway. And they are so concerned about that missing element that they send Peter and John down to the Samaritan city to take care of the omission.

What is it that's missing? The baptism in the Holy Spirit! Peter and John come down to the revival for one reason and one reason only—to lay hands on and pray for the new converts that they might receive the Holy Spirit, for as the scripture says,

> (The Holy Spirit) had not yet fallen on any of them, but they had only been baptized in the name of the Lord Jesus. Then they laid their hands on them and they received the Holy Spirit. —Acts 8:16-17

So again, we see quite clearly from scripture that the Holy Spirit operating in conversion is an altogether different, and prior, manifestation from the Holy Spirit's operation in the baptism in the Holy Spirit.

It is generally understood that the baptism in the Holy Spirit is an empowering experience which introduces the Christian into the supernatural realm of the Christian life. I believe the scriptural account of the Samaritan revival bears this out. There were supernatural signs and miracles in the

Samaritan revival, but obviously, they were taking place because of the anointing on Philip's ministry, since Philip was a man "full of the Holy Spirit" (Acts 6:3-5). It was the concern of the apostles that these new converts, who had met Jesus as Lord and Savior, should also experience Jesus as the Baptizer in the Holy Spirit, and so move into the same miraculous dimension of power which operated so vitally through Philip's ministry.

Acts 9:1-19
PAUL'S CONVERSION, HEALING, AND BAPTISM IN THE HOLY SPIRIT

The story in Acts nine reveals how Saul, who became Paul, was converted on the road to Damascus when he was struck down by a blinding light from heaven, right in the midst of his campaign to persecute Christians. Jesus spoke from the midst of the light saying, "Saul, Saul, why do you persecute me?" And Saul answered, "Who are you, Lord?" And the Lord said, "I am Jesus, whom you are persecuting." So Paul met Jesus on the road to Damascus in a most dramatic way. But while he was soundly converted in that experience, he was still not equipped with power for ministry. Therefore, God picked an obscure disciple named Ananias to come and pray for Paul, not only that his sight might be restored, but that he might "be filled with the Holy Spirit" (Acts 9:17).

Acts 10:1-46
THE HOUSEHOLD OF CORNELIUS CONVERTED AND BAPTIZED IN THE HOLY SPIRIT

Acts, chapter ten, contains the story of Peter being called to preach the gospel at the house of Cornelius. As Peter preaches the good news, those hearing are converted and are immediately baptized in the Holy Spirit with the confirming evidence of speaking in tongues. This account of the baptism in the Holy Spirit differs from the others in the book of Acts in one major particular. The time span between accepting Jesus as savior and subsequently receiving the baptism in the Holy Spirit is greatly condensed from a matter of weeks or days or hours to a matter of minutes.

On the day of Pentecost, it was ten days from the time Jesus promised the baptism in the Holy Spirit to his disciples until they received it. In Acts, chapter eight, it was also a matter of days from the time the new converts in Samaria were converted under Philip's preaching until Peter and John arrived to administer the baptism in the Holy Spirit. And in Acts, chapter nine, Paul's conversion on the road to Damascus took place three days before God sent Ananias to pray for him to receive his sight and be filled with the Holy Spirit.

According to Acts ten, Peter is preaching a Spirit-inspired sermon to the household of Cornelius, telling them about Jesus Christ. And when he reaches the point in his sermon where he proclaims forgiveness of sins for all who believe in Jesus (and the heart of the gospel is that Jesus Christ died to save sinners), the folk in Cornelius' home believe the message of salvation. Immediately, things begin to happen. Everyone who believes Peter's words is immediately baptized in the Holy Spirit. Even before Peter can conclude his sermon, "the Holy Spirit fell on all who heard the word" (Acts 10:44).

Acts 19:1-6
PAUL MINISTERS THE BAPTISM IN THE HOLY SPIRIT TO TWELVE DISCIPLES IN EPHESUS

The final story of the baptism in the Holy Spirit in the book of Acts relates how Paul discovers a small band of disciples of Jesus in Ephesus. Noticing something missing from their Christian experience, he asks, "Did you receive the Holy Spirit when you believed?" (Acts 19:2). By the very question he asks, Paul illustrates the truth we are stressing in this chapter—namely that conversion is one experience and baptism in the Holy Spirit is a separate, subsequent experience. We could restate Paul's question in a slightly different way and not strain its meaning at all. Paul was asking the Ephesian disciples, "Have you received the baptism in the Holy Spirit since you accepted Jesus Christ as your Savior?"

And when Paul discovers that not only have they not been baptized in the Holy Spirit, neither have they had Christian baptism in water, he takes care of both omissions. He baptizes them in water in the name of the Lord Jesus, then lays hands on them and prays for them to receive the baptism in the Holy

Spirit. The twelve men receive the baptism and begin praising God in tongues and prophesying.

Let us make this one final point concerning the two experiences. Everyone needs to see that conversion and baptism in the Holy Spirit are not only separate experiences—they are given for separate and distinct purposes. Conversion is that experience of Jesus Christ by which the *non-Christian* becomes a Christian, while the baptism in the Holy Spirit is that experience for the *Christian* to make him a powerful Christian. It is as simple as that.

Chapter 3

Tongues: The Primary Evidence of Baptism in the Holy Spirit

We said in chapter one that the church is in the midst of world-wide revival and that central to that revival is the experience we call the baptism in the Holy Spirit. Now, let us go a step further and state that central to the baptism in the Holy Spirit is a phenomenon called "glossolalia" or speaking in tongues. And, let's face it, speaking in tongues causes most of the controversy which continually swirls around the baptism in the Holy Spirit. As John Sherrill observed in his classic book, *They Speak With Other Tongues*, "Tongues make people fight." If it weren't for this particular (some would insist "peculiar") manifestation accompanying the baptism in the Holy Spirit, it would be far more readily received in many Christian circles.

The question is asked everywhere I go, "Why is there so much controversy over speaking in tongues?" Consistent experience in ministering the baptism has convinced me that there are two major reasons for the controversy. One is fear, the other is ignorance. The fear comes from years of dire warnings that speaking in tongues is "fanaticism, emotionalism or of the devil." And when these complaints have repeatedly bombarded the ears of earnest Christians who have never examined the Scriptures carefully for themselves, or heard clear scriptural teaching about the baptism in the Holy Spirit, the result is a deeply imbedded emotional prejudice against what God is doing in the church today.

We need to understand that it is Satan, not God, who stands to benefit most from the criticism and discrediting of spiritual gifts. And we need to recognize he is continually stirring up all the prejudice and false teaching he can against the provision God has made for us. Someone has said that the two words Satan seems to hate most are "tongues" and "demons." For speaking in tongues is the initial evidence of an experience designed to equip Christians with supernatural power with which to wage an effective battle against Satan, and the word "demon" brings to light and exposes the nasty little helpers Satan uses to torment the people of God and to undermine the works of God. No wonder Satan hates for Christians to become familiar and knowledgeable about either the supernatural gifts of the Holy Spirit or the cunning, hidden ways he uses to oppose the purposes of God.

Satan's favorite tactic is to throw up an emotional smokescreen, to create controversy and anger when the gift of speaking in tongues is mentioned. More than once I have seen sincere Christians cooperate amiably and peaceably with religious leaders who deny the Divinity of Christ, who scoff at the Word of God and who frankly and openly admit their rejection of the historic truths of the Christian faith. And I've seen these same Christians become livid with anger when some Christian acquaintance testifies to the baptism in the Holy Spirit with the evidence of speaking in tongues. Surely, it is not difficult to determine the source of such anger. It can scarcely be said to come from God.

Personally, I believe it is more than coincidence that the criticism of speaking in tongues *began within minutes after it first appeared on the Day of Pentecost.* When the 120 began speaking in tongues and the curious onlookers gathered, they were amazed to hear them praising God in languages they had never learned. Those onlookers knew something supernatural was taking place— at least those who heard and understood the languages (Acts 2:7-12).

But note that others standing by who did *not* understand any of the twelve or more languages the various disciples were using in their praise to God, tried to discredit the experience saying, "These men are a bunch of babbling drunks!" (Acts 2:13). So the devil didn't waste any time in trying to discredit the experience of speaking in tongues, and he's been trying to do the same thing ever since!

Fear and ignorance, combined with false teaching, have proved powerful weapons in Satan's hands. After I have taught on the place of speaking in tongues in relation to the baptism in the Holy Spirit, sometimes people will complain, "Why do you spend so much time talking about speaking in tongues?" The answer is simple—to try and generate a little light where before there's been mostly heat!

It's tongues that is the point of controversy. That's where the criticisms land. And the only way I know to clear up the criticisms and misconceptions about speaking in tongues is to provide scriptural teaching on the subject. Of course, for some people, *any* mention of speaking in tongues is too much.

I know a Spirit-baptized minister's wife who teaches Sunday School in her husband's church where people are very touchy about the charismatic movement and the baptism in the Holy Spirit. She chose one Sunday in the year to teach her Intermediate Sunday School class about the gifts of the Holy Spirit and speaking in tongues. She wisely chose Pentecost Sunday, when the scripture lesson dealt directly with the subject. The following Sunday she asked her pupils if any of them had discussed the lesson with their parents. One little boy said, "Yes, I told my parents and they said they are sick and tired of all this talk about 'speaking in tongues.'" So in that case, thirty minutes once a year was too much!

At a ministerial meeting in the town in Pennsylvania where I pastored several years ago, some of the ministers discussed speaking in tongues with me. (Word had spread through the community about a number of my church members receiving the baptism in the Holy Spirit and speaking in tongues.) From the totally negative (and unscriptural!) comments about speaking in tongues those ministers made, one would suppose God had made a horrible mistake on the Day of Pentecost when He sent speaking in tongues along as the evidence of the baptism in the Holy Spirit.

But I believe God knew exactly what He was doing on the day of Pentecost, that He did it right the very first time, and that He hasn't changed His mind since. I also believe it is the intent of God that every person receiving the baptism in the Holy Spirit today *should* experience the miracle of speaking in tongues.

Such an observation brings us to the next obvious question: "Does a person *have* to speak in tongues in order to receive the baptism in the Holy Spirit?" And by the critical way the question is often asked I can usually tell some skeptic has been busily at work warning the questioner about "fanaticism" or "emotionalism" or that "the devil can speak in tongues."

The answer to that question is, "You don't *have* to, you *get* to!" Speaking in tongues is a privilege. It is a precious gift from God. It is a new and intimate way of praying with direct, supernatural help. And the gifts of the Holy Spirit are not to be despised or criticized. Nor does God give gifts that are useless or "divisive."

Other critics of tongues say, "But the scriptures teach that not everyone is supposed to speak in tongues." And they quote Paul's statement in 1 Corinthians 12:30, "Do all speak in tongues?" And his instructions in 1 Corinthians 14:27, "If any speak in a tongue let there be only two or at most three…"

But Paul's teaching in those verses does not refer to the *ability* to speak in tongues which comes when one is baptized in the Holy Spirit. Paul is speaking of ministry gifts which God has set in the church, explaining that not all Spirit-baptized Christians have the same *ministry*, and also giving advice to Spirit-baptized Christians how, in a public worship service, tongues are to be ministered in a proper way and are to be properly interpreted.

Notice how Paul also says, "Now I want you *all* to speak in tongues…" (1 Corinthians 14:5). Obviously, Paul is not so inept as to say one thing one place and then contradict what he said a few verses earlier. Note too, that *at no time does Paul ever criticize speaking in tongues.* He only criticizes the misuse of the gift. Modern critics would do well to confine their criticisms in the same way. So, when we teach about the manifestation of tongues, a distinction needs to be made between the ability to pray in tongues which comes when one is baptized in the Holy Spirit, and the *ministry gift* of tongues which involves tongues in the public assembly which are to be interpreted. While all Christians should be baptized in the Holy Spirit with the evidence of speaking in tongues, not all will have a prominent *ministry* of speaking in tongues publicly.

But while we teach and fully expect everyone receiving the baptism in the Holy Spirit to speak in tongues, we admit not everyone does. Not because it's not God's will, but because of fear or ignorance they quench the Spirit. God will not force any child of His to do anything that child is not willing to do. Therefore, some people receive the baptism in the Holy Spirit—and their changed lives testify that they have received the baptism—but do not speak in tongues. At least, not at first.

Even the scriptures do not insist that everyone *must* speak in tongues at the time he receives the baptism. But clearly, it is the norm, since in four of the five cases in Acts where the Holy Spirit is received, the people receiving end up speaking in tongues. The only exception is the Samaritan revival in Acts eight where tongues are not specifically mentioned. But many Bible scholars feel that even on that occasion tongues were in evidence since Simon the magician "saw" something which made him want to buy the ability to transmit the baptism in the Holy Spirit (Acts 8:18-19). Many scholars agree that speaking in tongues was the evidence Simon "saw."

Personally, I am convinced that anyone who has received the baptism in the Holy

Spirit can—once he understands what is involved—speak in tongues, and that it is only his own fear or prejudice or lack of understanding which prevents it. Repeated experience has borne this out.

Recently I ministered to a group of about twenty persons after having taught about the baptism in the Holy Spirit. During the prayer time, all of them received the Holy Spirit and began praying freely and beautifully in other tongues. One young woman came to me afterward, eyes glistening with tears of gratitude, and said, "I want to thank you for proving to me what I already had was real." Then she explained how she had received prayer for the baptism in the Holy Spirit months before, in a church service where the minister had told the people to accept by faith that they had received and not to expect any outward manifestation. "But from the day I accepted it by faith," she added, "I noticed that every time I began to pray, strange foreign-sounding syllables would fill my mind, and I couldn't understand why. Repeatedly, I tried to dismiss them, but every time I prayed they were there. I know now it was the Holy

Spirit gently trying to lead me into the blessing of speaking in tongues."

Often in the audiences where I speak on this subject there will be some who feel they have received the baptism in the Holy Spirit but who have not received the manifestation of tongues. This may prompt them to ask the question, "Can you have the baptism in the Holy Spirit without speaking in tongues?"

I like Reverend Derek Prince's response to that question. He answers with another question: "Can an elephant be an elephant without a trunk?" The answer is, "Yes. But a trunkless elephant is a pretty funny-looking elephant." The trunk is a normal and important appendage for the elephant. He feeds himself with it—he bathes himself with it—in fact, without it he is not a normal elephant.

So it is with speaking in tongues in relation to the baptism in the Holy Spirit. Scripturally and practically it is an important part of the baptism. So, as you consider this teaching, if you happen to be a "trunkless elephant," or if you have friends who are, both you and they need to understand the significance of speaking in tongues, and to see that you and they are missing out on one of the major blessings which should accompany the baptism in the Holy Spirit. Briefly, some of the major reasons for receiving and manifesting tongues are:

1. According to scripture, it is God's will for everyone to speak in tongues since Paul says, "Now I want you all to speak in tongues…" (1 Corinthians 14:5).

2. Speaking in tongues strengthens and edifies the believer (1 Corinthians 14:4).

3. He who speaks in tongues is praying in the Spirit (1 Corinthians 14:15).

4. Speaking in tongues (praying in the Spirit) is a divinely-inspired means of praying effectively for others (Romans 8:26-27).

5. Speaking in tongues is the normal scriptural means of entering into the baptism in the Holy Spirit (Acts 2:4, 10:44-46, 19:6).

And for any "trunkless elephant" who may be reading this, let me give these words of encouragement: you *can* pray in tongues, and according to God's Word, you *should*. It is a part of your divine heritage as a believing Christian to enter into the supernatural life of God through the baptism in the Holy Spirit and its initial manifestation of speaking in tongues. Repeatedly, I have seen those Christians who felt they were baptized in the Holy Spirit but who had not spoken in tongues seek and receive tongues. Not one ever told me afterwards that he thought it was a mistake or a waste of time, but hundreds have testified to a new release of spiritual power in their lives as a result of beginning to pray in tongues.

We said earlier that many persons seem afraid to speak in tongues because they've been told that it's just emotionalism or fanaticism. That is another of Satan's favorite lies. He will do anything to discredit the gifts and graces of God. He will as quickly label speaking in tongues as emotionalism or fanaticism today as he labeled it drunken babbling on the day of Pentecost. Any lie will serve, as long as it dissuades people from believing and receiving the gifts of God.

The charge of "emotionalism" has caused many people to fear that they might "lose control of themselves" if they spoke in tongues, or that "God will make me do something which embarrasses me." But as we said before, the Holy Spirit does not *force* us to do anything. You can be sure that any spirit which *compels* you to do anything or say anything you do not want to say is not the Holy Spirit. People who are afraid that they might do something embarrassing or speak in tongues at the wrong time have failed to realize that the act of speaking in tongues is *always* under the control of the one speaking. The person, not the Holy Spirit, decides when he will speak out, and whether he will speak in tongues quietly or aloud. The very fact that Paul gives strict instructions about how and when speaking in tongues is to be manifested in a public meeting (1 Corinthians 14:27-28) clearly indicates that the one speaking is in control, for Paul's instructions would be worthless unless those he was teaching had the ability to obey his instructions.

Another objection often expressed about speaking in tongues as it happens today is that it isn't really supernatural like it was on the day of Pentecost. It is argued that at Pentecost the tongues were in languages understood by those present and listening, but today's tongues are just emotional gibberish, and can't be considered a divine manifestation at all.

But the truth is that today's speaking in tongues *is* miraculous and that many times the languages which are spoken *are* recognized— by other persons present—as foreign languages not naturally known by the one speaking. I could easily double the size of this book simply by setting out to record several dozen such incidents. But three brief illustrations should be sufficient.

A Christian friend in Texas, in whose home I was a guest recently, had this experience. She was sitting in a small Christian meeting, praying quietly in tongues while waiting for the service to begin. A Mexican-American friend sitting beside her heard the quiet flow of prayer and praise to God and nudged her excitedly.

"Sister, do you know you were speaking Spanish? You were saying, 'Now is the time to praise the Lord. Now is the time to praise the

Lord.'" Yet my Texas friend cannot speak a word of Spanish naturally.

Then, in a Full Gospel Business Men's Fellowship Chapter meeting in Ohio a few months ago, at the close of my message there were two manifestations of tongues followed by interpretations. Then there was a third manifestation of tongues which was not interpreted. But afterward, one of the officers of the chapter introduced me to an amazed young man who was visiting an FGBMFI meeting for the first time. He had recently returned from the war in Vietnam where he had served with Army Intelligence. Because he had learned the Vietnamese language, he had been used to interrogate prisoners. His amazement stemmed from the fact that the third person who had spoken in tongues in the meeting had prayed a beautiful prayer in Vietnamese although he had no natural knowledge of any foreign language whatever.

Also, there have been a number of reports of native Christians in foreign lands praising God in perfect English when they receive the baptism in the Holy Spirit. Of course, to them English would be an "unknown tongue," but known to the ministers and missionaries praying with them.

Yet, in spite of the obviously miraculous demonstration such incidents provide, we need to remember that, according to Scripture, *the validity of the experience of tongues is not dependent on the languages being understood.* For example, in Acts chapter ten, where Peter preaches to the household of Cornelius and the people accept Jesus as Savior and are immediately baptized in the Holy Spirit and begin speaking in tongues, there is no evidence that the tongues are in recognizable languages. Nevertheless, Peter, in reporting the incident to the apostles and brethren back in Jerusalem said, "the Holy Spirit fell on them just as on us at the beginning" (Acts 11:15). Obviously, Peter accepted the validity of the baptism in the Holy Spirit at Cornelius' house, not because the tongues were recognizable as they had been at Pentecost, but simply on the basis of the tongues themselves.

So, regardless of the many misleading and inaccurate statements made about speaking in tongues by its critics, both the Scriptures and current experience indicate that it is the normal introductory sign or evidence that one has received the baptism in the Holy Spirit and is of great spiritual value to all who receive and use it.

But what about those who've wanted to receive the baptism and speak in tongues, but somehow haven't been able to? Well, we'll be dealing with that problem in the next chapter.

Chapter 4

Tongues and the "Chronic Seeker"

If I were asked to name the greatest barrier to receiving the baptism in the Holy Spirit with the evidence of speaking in tongues, I would be obliged to say it is a lack of understanding about the way the miraculous power of God is released in the Christian's life. The principle involved is one which, when understood and applied, puts a person in the proper position to receive what God has promised. The principle is simply this: *The power of God is released by an act of faith on man's part.*

Before we apply this principle to receiving the baptism in the Holy Spirit with speaking in tongues, let us examine it in Scripture. One example is the story of the healing of the woman with the issue of blood (Matthew 9:19-22, Luke 8:43-48). As Jesus made his way toward her, surrounded by a crowd of people, the woman said to herself, "If I touch even his garment I shall be made well." When she managed to touch him, immediately Jesus stopped and said, "Who touched me?" Peter chided him, saying, "Master, the multitudes surround You and press upon You." But Jesus was insistent about a *particular* touch. "Someone touched me, for I perceive that power has gone forth from me," He said. And when they identified the woman, Jesus commended her saying, "Daughter, your faith has made you well, go in peace."

Now obviously, there were other needy people pressing against Jesus: the sick, the lame, the troubled. But the one who received the miracle was the woman who touched Him in faith. There was no miracle in her reaching out, and there was no power in Jesus' garment. But her seemingly irrational act, the foolish act of reaching out *in faith*, was the key to her healing. The power was there in Jesus all the time, but something was required of the woman before that power was released in her behalf. And it was the combination of what the woman did and what God did that gave her the healing. Her simple act of faith triggered the flow of God's power.

This same principle holds true when it comes to receiving the baptism in the Holy

Spirit with the evidence of speaking in tongues. I've seen the principle demonstrated repeatedly all over the United States and overseas as well. Once a person understands that he has a vital part to play in receiving the baptism in the Holy Spirit, it is a simple matter for him to receive. But without this understanding, and unless he is willing to act in faith, he may have great difficulty.

Many of those we've come to call "chronic seekers" receive the baptism and begin to speak in tongues in a matter of minutes after hearing the simple teaching which makes this principle clear.

Essentially, the baptism in the Holy Spirit is comprised of two parts: first, receiving the Holy Spirit by faith, and second, manifesting the Spirit's presence through speaking in tongues. Speaking in tongues is *not* the baptism in the Holy Spirit, but is the verbal expression or overflow of it. We can put it this way: If I ask any of you, "Are you a Christian? Are you saved?", you would respond by saying, "Yes, I have accepted Jesus Christ as my Savior." But your words are not your salvation, they are the vocal expression of your salvation. So it is with speaking in tongues. Tongues are *not* the baptism but they are the vocal *expression* of that baptism.

The principle that man must play an essential part in releasing the miraculous power of God in his life applies to the baptism in the Holy Spirit, especially in reference to receiving the evidence of speaking in tongues. Speaking in tongues *is* supernatural; it *is* miraculous. But like other miracles, it too is comprised of two parts: man's part and God's part. But many people have not understood this and have waited for God to do it all. They've never done their part, they've never reached out in faith, and hence, have never spoken in tongues.

Suppose the woman with the issue of blood had just stood wistfully to one side as Jesus passed and said, "Well, I sure wish the Lord Jesus would come over here and heal me." You can bet she wouldn't have received her healing. She had to reach out and press through to touch the Lord. And when she did all she could do, God did what he could do, and she was healed.

From repeated experience, I find this is the problem with most "chronic seekers," and most "trunkless elephants." When it comes to speaking in tongues, they have failed to reach out in faith. *They have been waiting for God to do what God was waiting for them to do.*

A few years ago I was speaking in a Pentecostal church in an Eastern city. My subject was the baptism in the Holy Spirit. At the close of the service, the minister gave an altar call for people who wanted the baptism. To my surprise, over twenty people responded. In those days, I had assumed that most members of Pentecostal churches had long since received the baptism in the Holy Spirit. I've since learned this isn't necessarily true. Many Pentecostal of Full Gospel churches offer little or no teaching on the baptism in the Holy Spirit, and many of their members have not had the experience.

Anyway, the minister pointed to an elderly man kneeling by the front pew. "See that man?" he asked me. "He's seeking the baptism. Would you go over and pray with him?"

So I went over and sat down on the pew where the man was kneeling and gave him just a few words of instruction about how we receive the Holy spirit by faith and then speak in tongues in faith. Then I said, "Now we'll pray that God will baptize you in the Holy Spirit and enable you to praise Him in other tongues. After I pray I want you to open your mouth in faith and begin to praise God in tongues."

We prayed and immediately the brother opened his mouth and began to speak in tongues, tears of joy streaming down his face. I returned to the minister and said, "Well, the brother received." To my surprise, the pastor began to jump up and down with excitement.

"He did? Are you sure?" And then he ran over to the brother and knelt down and listened to him praising God in tongues. Then the minister began to weep for joy.

I thought to myself, "This is an emotional bunch of Pentecostals I got mixed up with tonight." Then the pastor came back to me wiping the tears from his face with his handkerchief and explained.

"This brother's been seeking the baptism in the Holy Spirit *for twenty-seven years!*"

Do you see the point? For over a quarter of a century that devoted Christian man had been waiting for God to do what God had been waiting for him to do. Earnest, sincere man that he was, he didn't want to "fake anything." So he had never taken that step of faith.

"I don't want to open my mouth and speak—I want the Holy Spirit to speak through me!" I've heard many a chronic seeker wall himself off from the baptism in the Holy Spirit with that complaint. Let me say it again. The miracles of God are comprised of two parts: man's part and God's part. Speaking in tongues is that kind of miracle. And the miraculous part isn't the act of speaking; it's the language. *You* speak; the Holy Spirit provides "the utterance," the words, the syllables. *You* must speak the words the Holy Spirit provides. And if you don't open your mouth and begin to speak, there will be no speaking in tongues. Let me give you one more illustration and then we'll be ready for the actual instruction for those seeking the baptism.

A minister friend of mine was present when this incident took place and related it to me. The pastor of a small denominational church had been seeking the baptism in the Holy Spirit for several years without success. He was one of those "chronic seekers" we've been talking about, an earnest Christian brother who didn't want to "fake anything." Although he had been prayed over by many people many times, he still had not received. Nationally known evangelists had prayed for him, every charismatic speaker and evangelist who came to town had laid hands on him and prayed, but with no results. Yet the man was determined; he kept seeking.

One night in a small church, following a revival service, ministry was offered for those seeking the baptism in the Holy Spirit. My friend was present and saw this earnest pastor make his way to the front of the church. Reaching the altar he flung himself down on the floor and began to pray. No one went to minister to him personally because it never did any good. All his friends had worn themselves out praying with him.

But after a few minutes everyone was amazed to hear him begin to pray aloud in tongues in a beautiful, clear language. All the people around began to rejoice that the brother had finally received his heart's desire, and they listened gratefully as he continued to speak in tongues.

Then, to their surprise, the minister pushed himself up from the floor and said, "I don't want you people to get the wrong impression. I still don't have the baptism in the Holy Spirit. I'm not speaking in tongues, I'm just making up funny noises. I finally got so tired of waiting for the Holy Spirit to speak through me that I just decided to open my mouth and begin to babble out sounds. But that's not the Holy Spirit, that's me! I hate to disappoint all of you, but I still don't have the baptism in the Holy Spirit."

Then it was the minister's turn to be surprised, for there were three young Chinese college students sitting on the front pew of the church. They had been viewing the entire proceedings. One of them answered the minister.

"Brother, we hate to disappoint you, but you've been praising God in perfect Chinese for the last three minutes, and we have understood every word you said!"

See the point? Because of a lack of understanding about his part in the miracle of speaking in tongues, the minister had not only robbed himself of the experience for years, but when it finally happened, refused to accept it. All God had wanted was for the man to step out in faith, to open his mouth and begin to praise God with the sound of his voice so the Holy Spirit could furnish him with a new language of praise. This is exactly what happened on the day of Pentecost.

> And they were all filled with the Holy Spirit and began to speak in other tongues as the Spirit gave them utterance.
>
> —Acts 2:4

Time and again I've had people read that scripture aloud. Then I would ask them, "Who began to speak in tongues?" And they would usually reply, "The Holy Spirit began to speak." But they are wrong. The Holy Spirit did *not* speak. The 120 spoke. "*They* were filled…and began to speak…as the Spirit gave them utterance (furnished the words)."

The Holy Spirit doesn't speak in tongues, *you* speak. And it is the combination of *you* speaking the words and syllables which the *Holy Spirit* furnishes that makes up the miracles of speaking in tongues.

And that is exactly what finally happened to our "chronic seeker," the earnest devoted minister we've been talking about. When he finally became desperate enough to open his mouth and begin to praise God with what he thought were meaningless sounds, that's all the help the Holy Spirit needed. He began to pour the Chinese language through the man's lips.

Chapter 5

Instructions For Receiving

(Note: This chapter is an actual transcription of instructions which have been given to numerous groups presenting themselves as candidates for the baptism in the Holy Spirit.)

Now, I'm assuming all of you are here in the prayer room because you are seeking the baptism in the Holy Spirit with the evidence of speaking in tongues. Am I right? Or, perhaps a few of you feel you have already received the baptism but have not spoken in tongues, and you are here to receive prayer for that...Yes, I see several of you are in that category. Well, I'm glad you're here because you *can* receive tongues and it *will* be an added blessing to you.

There is only one major prerequisite to receiving the baptism in the Holy Spirit: You must have already accepted Jesus Christ as your personal Savior. Anyone here who has not made that commitment should be in the other prayer room where ministry is being offered to those seeking salvation. Is there anyone here who has not made that prior commitment?

Well, since no one raised a hand, I assume that you are all Christians, and thus, proper candidates for the baptism.

Now the first thing I want to tell you is this: You can sit back and relax, for you *can* receive the baptism in the Holy Spirit and you *can* speak in tongues. It is in your power to do all you have to do. The same faith that enabled you to receive Jesus Christ as your Savior is all the faith you need to receive the baptism in the Holy Spirit with speaking in tongues. After all, in one sense, the baptism is simply receiving more of Jesus. It's meeting Him in a new dimension, as the Baptizer in the Holy Spirit as John the Baptist spoke of Him in Luke 3:16. There is no reason why every one of you will not receive the Holy Spirit and be praising God in a new and unknown tongue within a very few minutes. So relax and be confident. It will happen.

I want to take a few minutes to explain the procedure we are going to follow. For purposes of instruction I find it helpful to divide the experience into two parts. The first step is receiving the Holy Spirit within; the second is to manifest the Spirit's presence by praising God in a new or "unknown" tongue. Again, let me make it clear; *everyone of you can do this*. It is within your power, once you understand what is required of you, to receive the Holy Spirit and to speak in tongues.

Now when the prayer for you to receive is offered (and I'm simply going to pray one single prayer aloud in behalf of all of you, asking the Lord Jesus to baptize you in the Holy Spirit and to enable you to praise Him in a new, supernatural way), immediately after the ending of that prayer, I will ask you to do a very simple thing. I will ask you to open your mouth and breathe in or drink in a deep, full breath of air.

There's a good reason for doing this. First, this breathing in or drinking in a breath of air provides a physical stimulus to your faith. Not only that, there is a kind of unique relationship between "breath" and "spirit." The word for "breath" is the same as the word for "spirit" in Greek and Hebrew, the two languages the New Testament was written in. And when Jesus prophesied the coming of the Holy Spirit at Pentecost He said:

> If anyone thirst, let him come to me and drink. He who believes in me...'Out of his heart shall flow rivers of living water.' Now this He said about the Spirit, which those who believed would receive; for as yet the Spirit had not yet been given, for Jesus was not yet glorified. —John 7:37-39

So this breathing in, or drinking in the Holy Spirit had scriptural endorsement. Therefore, when I give the word to open your mouth and breath in, as you do it, *believe* that the Spirit is coming into your life in a new way, a more powerful way. I believe it. I've seen it happen to so many people in the past few years, that I *know* what is going to happen. I *know* you will receive. I believe God *always* answers the prayer of the Christian who is seeking the baptism in the Holy Spirit.

But it is important to realize that you receive the Holy Spirit by faith and not by feeling. So while some of you may experience some deep or powerful emotion as the Spirit breaks in on you in this new way, others—and I dare say most others—will not feel anything.

Sometimes people experience a deep awareness of the love and presence of God, others experience joy and still others are moved to tears. And if such feelings come, welcome them; but don't be concerned if they do not. Most of you may experience no emotion at all, and that is perfectly all right. It seems that most people receiving the Holy Spirit today, receive quietly and without undue emotion. The important thing is not what you feel but what you believe. Believe the Holy Spirit is coming in, because it is true. He is.

All right. That's the first step; "breathing in" the Holy Spirit and having faith that He's coming in. And that is the easiest of the two steps. But we don't want to stop there; we also want you to have the Scriptural confirmation of the Holy Spirit's presence in your life in a new way by having you receive the manifestation of speaking in tongues. Again, let me tell you, relax! You *can* do this. You *can* receive the evidence of speaking in tongues. It is in your power to do it. Let me explain what I mean.

Speaking in tongues—which is the scriptural proof or sign that you have received the baptism in the Holy Spirit—is a miracle; it is supernatural. I believe we are all agreed on that. But let me remind you again that miracles are comprised of two parts: man's part (which is natural) and God's part (which is supernatural.) One of the best Scriptural examples of this truth is the miracle of Peter walking on the water, recorded in Matthew chapter fourteen. You remember the story.

Jesus comes walking on the water toward the boat containing his disciples. Peter calls out, "Lord, if it is you, bid me come to you on the water." The Lord replies, "Come." And the Scriptures tell us, "Peter got out of the boat and walked on the water and came to Jesus" (Matthew 14:29).

Several years ago, the Holy Spirit showed me something about that miracle which has been a big help. He showed me that Peter walking on the water was the same kind of miracle we experience when we speak in tongues. You see, Peter's miracle, like speaking in tongues, was comprised of two parts: Peter's part and God's part.

Now, what was Peter's part in the miracle? Simply to get out of the boat and walk, that's all. In other words, *Peter was not required to do anything supernatural.* All he had to do was get out of the boat and walk, in exactly the same way he would have done if the boat had been pulled up on the shore. There was nothing supernatural about Peter walking. It was just the simple, physical act of walking in obedience to the Lord's invitation to come to Him.

Speaking in tongues is like that. When the time comes for you to speak in tongues, you are to open your mouth and begin to speak, just like Peter stood up and stepped out of the boat and began to walk. Now, I see some of you looking a little puzzled, but stay with me. Remember how, when Peter stepped over the side of the boat and began to walk, he had fulfilled his part of the miracle. And when he began his act of walking in faith, God was right there to do His part. It was Peter's job to walk, *it was God's job to hold him on top of the waves.* That was the supernatural part of the event. The miracle wasn't that Peter walked, but that he didn't sink! And it was a combination of Peter walking and God holding him up that made the miracle. Every time Peter's foot hit the water, God was there to hold him up.

Speaking in tongues is like that. The miracle of speaking in tongues isn't *that* you speak, it's *what* you speak. The act of speaking is a natural, physical act, just like Peter's act of walking was a natural, physical act. And when you open your mouth to begin to speak, to praise God with the sound of your voice, the Holy Spirit will provide you with the words, the syllables, the phrases with which to do it. Let me say it again: the miracle in speaking in tongues isn't in the act of speaking, it's in the language that's given you to speak. And it is the combination of *you* speaking out the words that the *Holy Spirit* provides which creates the miracle of speaking in tongues, just as it was the combination of Peter's stepping out of the boat and walking, while God held him up, that created the miracle of walking on the water.

The only way Peter could discover that he could walk on the water was to step out of the boat and begin to walk; and the only way you will ever speak in tongues is to open your mouth and begin to speak. I am confident that thousands of people who have earnestly but unsuccessfully sought the baptism in the Holy Spirit with the evidence of speaking in tongues have fallen short right at this point. They have been unwilling to "get out of the boat." Or at least, they were ignorant of the act of faith which is required of them in order to receive the evidence of speaking in tongues. I know this is true because I've prayed with many such people myself. And the breakthrough always comes once they grasp the principle that the Holy Spirit is not going to "speak through them," and that they themselves must open their mouths and begin to speak.

So when the time comes for you to speak in tongues, be ready! After I have prayed the prayer in your behalf, and immediately after you have opened your mouth and breathed in the Holy Spirit, I'm going to tell you to let that breath out. Only, do not let it out silently; put the sound of your voice behind it. Just begin to praise God with the sound of your voice as if you never learned the English language. God already knows you can speak English, so don't even attempt to praise Him in your natural language. If you start to pray or praise in English, you'll only have to stop before you can begin to speak in tongues. Even the Holy Spirit cannot make you speak two languages at once.

So make up your mind, right now, that you will praise God only with the sound of your voice, and with the words and syllables which the Holy Spirit will provide. From the moment you open your mouth to praise God in this new way, words and syllables will be right there on the tip of your tongue with which to praise Him. Not English words, but strange, funny-sounding words and syllables which make no sense at all to your mind. Now I use the word "funny-sounding" intentionally, because that is just exactly what they will sound like in your mind. But remember, they are words and syllables in a new, "unknown" tongue, so how could they sound anything else but "funny-sounding?" Remember how Paul said, "If I pray in a tongue, my spirit prays, but my mind is unfruitful" (1 Corinthians 14:14). You see, speaking in tongues originates, not in your mind, but in your spirit, inspired by the Holy

Spirit. It is a way of releasing your spirit in free worship to God, without having the worship pass through the limiting bottleneck of your understanding. It is prayer *in the Spirit*, not prayer with the understanding.

The baptism in the Holy Spirit with speaking in tongues is not designed to do anything for your intellect. It is a spiritual experience, designed to liberate your spirit in worship and to move you into a new dimension of Christian experience which the mind or intellect cannot normally accept. Miracles never make sense to the natural mind. Neither does speaking in tongues.

So when I give the word, I want you to open your mouth and begin to praise God with the sound of your voice as if you never learned the English language. Just become like little children who communicate with their parents with sounds and syllables. In fact, the more childlike you become, the easier it is for the Holy Spirit to have His way.

Now when I give the word for you to open your mouth and begin to praise God, I know from experience that some of you will receive tongues instantly. Others will be a little hesitant to begin to speak. But just gather your courage and begin to speak anyway. Just babble out whatever pops into your mind or whatever you feel on your lips and tongue. And once you begin, keep it up. Don't stop. Let the language flow out freely. If you can speak five words or syllables, you can speak five thousand. The Holy Spirit has an unlimited vocabulary.

And another thing. When you start to speak, don't worry about what it sounds like. It may sound like Chinese, like Polynesian, like the notes of the musical scale, or even like baby talk. What it sounds like is the Holy Spirit's business. Your business is just to speak out. The Holy Spirit will give you words and syllables in the language He wants you to pray in. Don't get concerned if the person sitting next to you is praying with different sounds than yours. Don't examine it, just do it!

When I ask you to open your mouth and begin to speak, I'm going to begin to speak in tongues aloud, along with you, just to encourage you. And then I may move around among you to listen to you and to encourage the slow ones. But don't wait for me to come and lay hands on your head or pray with you personally. Just move out in faith and begin to praise God.

Now, I believe it's time to pray. Relax, and get ready for what is going to happen. You are about to move into a deep and wonderful new dimension of Christian experience, even though it happens in what may seem to be a strange and foolish way. Never mind. It's real. It's supernatural. And believe me, after today, your life will never be the same! Let's pray.

Dear Jesus, we thank You for the promise of Your Holy Spirit today. We thank You that You are pouring out Your Holy Spirit with the blessing of speaking in tongues. Lord, we ask You to honor the faith of all the people in this room, and to confirm Your Word in them. We ask you right now, Lord Jesus, to baptize everyone in this room with Your Holy Spirit, and enable them to praise You with a language they never learned but which is pleasing to You. Thank You, Lord Jesus, Amen.

Now, everyone of you, "Receive ye the Holy Ghost" and praise God in other tongues! Amen!

All right, open your mouth and take in that deep breath of air. Breathe in deeply and, as you do, believe the Holy Spirit is coming in. That's right! Good!

Now, let that breath out, and begin to praise God with the sound of your voice, and receive the utterance the Holy Spirit gives.

Note: On the occasion from which this transcription was made, over one hundred people received the baptism in the Holy Spirit and began speaking in tongues. The time of prayer and rejoicing continued for some fifteen or twenty minutes. Then before the congregation was dismissed, those newly baptized in the Holy Spirit were given these final words of advice:

All right. It appears that practically everyone in the room has received the baptism, and I can tell that most of you are worshiping in the new language given to you by God.

But before we leave, I want to make a few suggestions:

1) What you are doing is new and strange and some of you are already having a few doubts. You are saying to yourselves, "Is this really it? Am I really speaking in tongues? Is this really the baptism in the Holy Spirit?"

And the answer is *yes*! What's happened to you is real! Jesus has just baptized you in the Holy Spirit and you are really speaking in tongues, no matter how strange you may feel. Everybody has doubts. That is to be expected. Just don't give in to them. Doubts are from the devil and are a sure-fire indication that you've got the real thing. The devil wouldn't try to talk you out of it if what you received wasn't real.

2) Some of you are much more fluent in your praying than others, and this is to be expected, too. To those of you who have spoken only a few words, let me make this suggestion: Once you get home and are alone, where no one else can hear, pull out all the stops. Open your mouth and praise God aloud, reaching out in faith for a larger vocabulary. You may tell God something like this: "Lord, I don't understand all that's happened, but I accept it in faith. I'm

determined to praise You in this new way! I'm going to open my mouth and praise You with these strange sounds and syllables, and I want You to give me more and more of them to praise You with."

3) Since you are in the midst of a new experience—since you have just entered into a new dimension in Jesus Christ—it is important that you become established in your new spiritual life. You must learn to stand firm on your new territory. Here's one way to do that:

Every day for the next two weeks, whenever you pray in English, give the Lord equal time praying in tongues. If you've been praying for thirty minutes each morning, starting tomorrow, pray half the time in English and spend the other half praising God in the Spirit, in tongues. Or better still, double your prayer time and spend thirty minutes praying each way.

Paul says in 1 Corinthians 14:15, "I will pray with the spirit and I will pray with the mind also…" Praying with the spirit is praying in tongues; praying with the mind is praying in your normal way, in English. Both are essential and Paul insists we should make room for both of them.

Praying in tongues will never take the place of your English praying, but it is a wonderful addition to it. Not only that, you don't have to concentrate on praying in the spirit, at least not after you get accustomed to it. You can just turn loose and let it flow. You can do it while driving your car, while sitting at your desk, working around the house, or even while talking with your friends. It is rather like a little engine deep inside. Once cranked up it can run almost continuously. In 1 Thessalonians 5:17, Paul says, "Pray without ceasing." I believe Paul was referring to praying in tongues since that's the only way I know anyone can actually pray without ceasing. But in the spirit, in tongues, it can be done. You can pray in tongues, even in your sleep, for your spirit never sleeps.

More than once I've been told by both husbands and wives how, after they received the baptism in the Holy Spirit, their spouses found out by waking up in the night and hearing them praying in tongues in their sleep.

So *practice* this new way of praying which Jesus has given you. Exercise the gift! Make a large, large place for it in your spiritual life, and God will richly bless you in its use!

But you, beloved, build yourselves up on your most holy faith; pray in the Holy Spirit; keep yourselves in the love of God... —Jude 20-21

The following letter of testimony was received from Reverend and Mrs. Dick Coleman of the Westside Baptist Church, Leesburg, Florida.

"Dear Brother Don,

"The Lord impressed us to write to you and share three beautiful, and yet rather unusual, experiences three persons we know have had while reading your new book, *Ministering the Baptism in the Holy Spirit* (former title of *Spiritual Power*).

"We have a dear brother who attends our church who is seventy-two or seventy-three years old. He has spent most of his weekends and vacations ministering to the Seminole Indians for the last thirty years. He received a healing of his heart during meetings with us last summer. In his quiet way, he has searched for the baptism in the Holy Spirit.

"Several weeks ago, after the morning service, he came to us and shared a beautiful testimony. He was reading your book, and when he came to the last page, the last line and the last word, God gloriously baptized him in the Holy Spirit. He said, 'I was just sitting in my chair reading and the Holy Spirit enveloped me and I started speaking in tongues.'

"This was shared at a prayer group, and two other people bore witness to similar experiences. One girl testified she sent the book to her brother who thought he had received but had only a few words in tongues. He called her long distance and said, 'When I got to the last page, the last line and the last word, I was truly immersed in the Spirit and began to speak in tongues fluently...'

"Afterward, he gave the book to another sister, not sharing how he had received, and she called several days later, rejoicing, saying when she got to the last page, the last line and the last word, God baptized her in the Holy Spirit with fluency in tongues.

"We're sure you've probably heard other testimonies similar to these by now, but we felt led of the Holy Spirit to share these with you.

"This book has meant a great deal to each of us, and there is a great need in the Body of Christ for this teaching.

"Much love in Jesus to you and your family,

Dick and Mignon Coleman"

Chapter 6

After The Baptism...What?

To move into a deeper spiritual dimension is not only to receive new blessings from God, but also to face new problems. This seems especially true when we consider the baptism in the Holy Spirit. A primary problem is that some Christians just don't understand what God is doing.

On the day of Pentecost, God poured out His Spirit on the 120 gathered in the upper room, and they all began to speak in tongues. The sight and sound of those Spirit-filled believers engaged in supernatural worship quickly caused a crowd to gather, and almost as quickly that crowd became divided into two camps. Some who witnessed the disciples praising God in languages they had never learned believed God was doing something wonderful and miraculous, "We hear them telling in our tongues the mighty works of God" (Acts 2:11); while others, mocking and unbelieving said, "They are filled with new wine" (Acts 2:13).

People haven't changed much in twenty centuries. The same misunderstanding over God's supernatural manifestations which divided the multitude on the day of Pentecost still divides the church today.

Some People Won't Understand

Once you receive the baptism in the Holy Spirit with the evidence of speaking in tongues, you become a member of a distinguished, but controversial, band of believers in Jesus Christ now numbering in the tens of millions. Unfortunately, millions of other good Christians are still asleep to the mighty outpouring of God's Holy Spirit, and they won't be able to accept what has happened to you, no matter what! Every Christian receiving the baptism in the Holy Spirit needs to be prepared for some misunderstanding.

If you are a member of a denominational church, you immediately encounter the difficulty of interpreting a *new* Christian experience to *old* Christian friends. Most Christians greatly admire certain other Christians; a popular minister, a respected Sunday School teacher, or some friend with deep Christian convictions who evidences a real degree of Christian maturity.

Therefore, it is both natural and understandable that upon receiving the Holy Spirit they long to share their experience with those "spiritual" friends, blithely assuming their testimony will be warmly welcomed. Alas! The painful experience of many Christians proves this is not the case.

Years ago, when I was still in Bible college, we began a small charismatic group on the campus, and some of the students received the baptism in the Holy Spirit. One girl, a candidate for the mission field, received the baptism and was filled with exuberant love and joy as a result of her experience. From the moment she received, everything seemed wonderfully changed. She went around the campus with stars in her eyes, praising God for everything.

A few days after her experience, she asked me if it would be all right for her to share her testimony with the professor for whom she worked as a part-time secretary.

"I don't think you should, Harriet," I cautioned. "That professor is a fine Bible scholar, but in the class I have with him, he has publicly stated that he doesn't believe miracles can happen today. I don't think he will understand if you try to tell him what happened to you."

But the girl's enthusiasm remained undiminished. "Oh, I'm certain he will! He's just like a father to me! Besides, he knows I've been unusually happy these last few days. He'll understand! After all, it's in the Bible, and I *know* he believes the Bible!"

No amount of pleading on my part could dissuade her from giving her testimony to the professor. The next time I saw her, her sad countenance and the misery in her eyes spoke eloquently of his reaction. Not only did he reject her testimony completely ("Are you claiming you are more spiritual than I am?") but also proceeded to condemn her soundly for "getting involved with a bunch of fanatics!"

As a result, she not only lost her joy but ended up totally renouncing her own experience, withdrawing from the charismatic fellowship and plunging into a time of deep spiritual depression and confusion.

The moral of this little story is: Many people don't understand, so be careful with whom you share your testimony! People you think are so spiritually mature that they will welcome what you have to say often prove to be the very ones who will reject it the most vehemently. Countless numbers of new charismatics have had the humbling experience of watching their own pastors react with indifference or even hostility to their testimony. I certainly do not agree with such reactions, yet, having been a pastor myself for over ten years, I do understand some of the reasons why they react.

Try to understand the average preacher's predicament. He has the spiritual responsibility for the whole congregation, not just for the few who are spiritually zealous. Generally, he's overworked and frustrated by more responsibility than he can adequately handle. Also, he is the recipient of constant "free advice" from church members who aren't completely satisfied with the way he's running things.

What's more, he's probably heard numerous rumors about "wild-eyed charismatic fanatics who split churches." Now, you come to him all starry-eyed with your testimony about a wonderful new experience which has revolutionized your life, implying—by the tone of your voice, if not by your actual words—that his problems would all be solved if only *he* would receive what *you* have received.

Even though all your testimony says and implies is true (indeed, the baptism in the Holy Spirit *is* a life-transforming experience and, indeed, he *does* need it!), he's in no position to hear or receive what you say. He may feel what you are talking about is more of a threat than a blessing. Is it any wonder, then, that he reacts with coolness or even hostility to your experience? So, when you receive the baptism in the Holy Spirit and want to share it with "spiritual friends," remember: *some people will not understand, no matter what!*

What can we do about that? Well, we'll discuss that problem next.

Live Your Experience, Don't Preach It!

Misunderstanding about the baptism in the Holy Spirit is difficult to handle, especially when it is rejected by your preacher or your church. But it can be a much greater problem when it happens right in your own family. My wife and I were unusually blessed in the fact that we received the baptism in the Holy Spirit at exactly the same time. Unfortunately, this is not usually the case. More often than not, either the wife or husband will receive before their spouse does, and the ensuing days, months or even years when one "has it" and the other "doesn't have it" can be most difficult.

More than one husband has actually threatened to have his wife committed to a mental institution simply because she has received the baptism. Many more have secretly felt their wives *should* be committed. Some wives have taken the children and moved out because their husbands received the baptism, claiming that their husbands had become so "fanatical" they were no longer safe to be around.

While such extreme reactions are not common, they do illustrate the tension and difficulty which can arise in a marriage where one has the baptism and the other does not. Frankly, I believe in the majority of cases, the major portion of the blame rests with the one who has *received* the blessing! A sound word of advice which fits both husbands and wives whose mates have not yet received the baptism in the Holy Spirit is: *live your experience; don't preach it!*

I cannot number the times a wife or a husband has come to me after some meeting to plead, "Please pray for my husband/wife! He/she is not interested in spiritual things!" Then, if I have time to listen, they will launch into a sad story of how hard it is to be a Spirit-baptized Christian when their mate rejects their experience.

While I understand and sympathize with anyone caught in such a situation, I have also come to feel sympathetic for the "unspiritual" one in the marriage. I've discovered that an unsatisfactory condition turns into a truly unbearable situation by the lack of wisdom and patience, not on the part of the one who *doesn't* have the baptism, but on the part of the one who *does!* If the baptism in the Holy Spirit hasn't made you more loving and attentive, if it hasn't made you more sensitive to the needs of your mate and more patient with his or her problems, then you've been ignoring part of what the baptism in the Holy Spirit is all about.

An increased measure of the Holy Spirit *should* result in a more Christ-like attitude on our part toward the faults and weaknesses in our mates. Yet, it seems that almost the opposite effect often appears. Enamored of our new experience and so caught up in the wonder and power of the *gifts* of the Holy Spirit, we fail to allow the *fruit* of the Spirit to develop. "To whom much is given, much shall be required," Jesus said (Luke 12:48). Yet many of us, after the baptism, act as if the more *we* are given, the more that is required of our wives or husbands! The problem of charismatic Christians trying to nag or preach their spouses into the baptism in the Holy Spirit is almost universal. Unfortunately, the only thing such zeal ever accomplishes is to push their mates further from what God desires for them.

At times I've told super-spiritual husbands, "Stop going to so many meetings and stay home more with your wife and children. Let the baptism in the Holy Spirit make you a better husband and father." Some of those pious husbands are the same ones who, before they were saved and baptized in the Holy Spirit, neglected their wives and children for bowling, golfing, or fishing. Now they neglect them saying, "My wife and children aren't interested in spiritual things."

And some super-spiritual wives who neglect their homes to come to meetings and plead for prayer for their husbands were inadequate homemakers *before* they received the baptism in the Holy Spirit. Now they neglect home and husband all the more, trotting from prayer meeting to prayer meeting. Is it any wonder their husbands remain unimpressed with their spirituality?

Without meaning to, some wives who tended to nag their husbands before receiving the Holy Spirit nag them even more afterward. Only now, since it is "sanctified" nagging, how can the poor husband fight back? No matter what he says or does, he's wrong because his wife is so spiritual! Not long ago, I had a conversation with a disgruntled charismatic wife who had such resentment against her husband that she was actually contemplating a divorce, simply because he would not seek the baptism in the Holy Spirit! Wives, remember that regardless of your baptism in the Holy Spirit, God still considers your husband the head of the house and wants you to be submitted to him in every way possible. The baptism in the Holy Spirit gives no woman justification for rebellion against her husband's leadership or for trying to usurp her husband's authority.

I'll say it again, both to husbands and wives; "Don't preach! Don't nag! Don't look or act pious! Don't leave little devotional books around the house in conspicuous places! Don't neglect your mate for an endless string of spiritual meetings! *Live out your baptism in the Spirit* in front of your spouse. Let him or her see the difference, not in what you say, but in how you live!"

I know a certain young Christian wife whose home situation was a hellish nightmare. Her husband was unsaved, and he neglected her and the children. She had retreated into a behavior pattern which alternated between explosions of violent temper and sullen withdrawal. The home was like a battleground.

In desperation, the young woman sought help from God, who graciously baptized her in the Holy Spirit. Overwhelmed by God's goodness and somehow finding more wisdom than most Christians seem to find, she determined to show her gratitude to God by becoming the best wife possible. She began to lavish attention on her surly husband.

She made it a point to refrain from nagging criticism, and while unable to completely control her outbursts of temper, she would quickly apologize afterward. Inwardly, she continued to praise God for what He had done for her, and to ask Him to save her husband.

Her tactics brought results. The more attention she paid to her husband, the less surly he became. She found him watching her in puzzlement as she cheerfully worked around the house. *Still, she said nothing!* One night, about six weeks after her baptism in the Holy Spirit, as they sat at supper, her husband suddenly put down his fork and looked at his wife with tears in his eyes.

"I don't understand what has happened to you, honey," he said brokenly. "But you've changed in some wonderful way, and I want whatever it is that you have found. Will you pray for me?" That very night he accepted Jesus Christ as his Savior, and a month later he too received the baptism in the Holy Spirit. Now true Christian peace reigns in that home.

How did it all come about? Through the wisdom of a wife who had the courage to *live* her experience rather than to preach it.

Be Aware of the Dangers in the Realm of the Spirit

There is a law in physics which states, "For every action there is a corresponding reaction." This law also operates in the realm of the Spirit. For every manifestation of the power of God, there seems to be a corresponding reaction on the part of Satan. When Jesus was baptized in the river Jordan by John, He also received the baptism in the Holy Spirit, the scriptures testifying that the Spirit descended upon Him like a dove. Immediately, He was led into the wilderness for a dramatic confrontation with Satan! We should remember that we are no better than Jesus. Soon after His baptism in the Holy

Spirit, every Christian will face trials and testings by the enemy.

Strangely enough, the average Christian receiving the baptism seems to have the idea that it insulates him from enemy attack! This spiritually adolescent point of view is far removed from the truth. Once in the supernatural realm of the Spirit, we receive not only impressions from the Holy Spirit but the harassment of enemy activity, as well.

A friend of mine received the baptism in the Holy Spirit some years ago with an immediate effect on his life and ministry. His father, a mature pastor with years of experience, noted his son's fresh spiritual exuberance. Drawing him aside, he asked bluntly, "Charles, have you been speaking in tongues?"

His son answered truthfully, "Yes, Dad, I've received the baptism of the Holy Spirit."

His father replied with these sobering words, "I know you're all excited about the powerful spiritual realm you've entered, son. But remember this; you're just a newborn babe in that realm, but Satan has been at home there for thousands of years!"

Those words of caution are sound advice for every Christian receiving the baptism in the Holy Spirit. While we would do nothing to dampen the ardor or appreciation for the blessings which become available through the baptism, we must clearly emphasize that there are also dangers to be recognized and pitfalls to be avoided once we enter the supernatural realm of the Spirit.

I believe that in His wisdom God allows every blessing we receive from Him to be challenged and tested by the devil. Since Satan is a thief and a robber, it is understandable that he will attempt to steal or destroy everything we get from God. And God allows him that right. We are not shielded from enemy attacks simply because we can speak in tongues. True, we have powerful spiritual weaponry with which to repel the satanic attack, but those attacks will come. Our new experience will be tested. After all, it is only those experiences proven under test and trial that are worth keeping. Let's list some ways Satan may become active after you receive the baptism in the Holy Spirit.

1) He will try to talk you out of the baptism in the Holy Spirit.

We mentioned earlier in the book how, when you first begin to speak in tongues, it is natural to have doubts about it. Let us stress the problem once more, here.

Once, in a Presbyterian church in northern Florida, I prayed for a group of twenty-five people to receive the baptism in the Holy Spirit with what I believed to be 100 percent success. One strikingly handsome woman in her late forties seemed especially fluent in tongues as she prayed. I remember her particularly because she had beautiful prematurely gray hair which seemed to frame her face like a silver halo.

At the close of the prayer time, we all left the chapel and headed down a long corridor toward the door leading to the parking lot. I happened to fall in behind this woman and two of her friends who were happily testifying to having received the Holy Spirit. Imagine my surprise when I heard this woman remark to her friends in a wistful voice, "I don't know what's wrong with me. I try and try, but I just can't seem to receive the Holy Spirit!"

I was stunned! I stepped in front of the ladies right there in the middle of the corridor and confronted the woman.

"Sister," I said, "what do you think was going on back there in that chapel when you were praying so fluently in tongues? Don't you know that those tongues were God's divine sign that you have received the baptism in the Holy Spirit?"

"Oh, I don't believe anything really happened to me," she lamented. "I just got caught up in the excitement and made a bunch of funny noises with my mouth. I don't really believe that was speaking in tongues. Besides, I don't *feel* any different. I don't understand why God baptizes others with His Spirit, yet I never seem to receive!"

There, in the middle of the church corridor, I lectured her for a few minutes, reminding her how the devil always tries to get us to deny what God has done. Then we returned to the chapel to pray again. This time she admitted that she felt the power of God and confessed that she now believed she had really been speaking in tongues.

We must understand that Satan is out to rob us of every blessing God gives! Many people have been seriously hampered in their spiritual growth by listening to Satan's lies. Let me suggest that if you must doubt something, don't doubt your experience from God, rather doubt your doubts about your experience!

2) The devil may personally torment you after you receive the baptism in the Holy Spirit.

After receiving the baptism in the Holy Spirit, many people are shocked to discover that their struggle against sin and temptation seems more fierce than ever. Often, all kinds of unpleasant and sinful thoughts which they felt they had already conquered as Christians suddenly reappear to harass them.

"I thought I was rid of my nasty temper until I received the Holy Spirit," one man testified to me only recently. "But now, every time I try to pray or witness I feel that explosive temper rising up inside. It frightens me."

Others have made confessions like this: "I never recall having an undue amount of lustful thoughts before, but since I received the baptism in the Holy Spirit, I find that every time I try to pray or read my Bible my mind is suddenly filled with obscene thoughts! What can I do?"

First, let us assure the people who confront such problems that their situation is not unnatural. The fact is, not a few Christians receiving the baptism in the Holy Spirit have latent demonic problems which cause little difficulty until the power of the Holy Spirit comes flooding into their lives. When the Holy Spirit comes in with power, the devil is often stampeded into the open! In Luke, chapter four, we read where Jesus came into the synagogue in Capernaum and a man who was worshiping there suddenly went berserk under the influence of a demon.

> And in the synagogue there was a man who had the spirit of an unclean demon; and he cried out with a loud voice, "Ah! What have you to do with us, Jesus of Nazareth? Have you come to destroy us? I know who you are, the Holy One of God!" —Luke 4:33-34

Apparently the man had deep-rooted demonic problems in his life which never surfaced until Jesus, full of the Holy Spirit, came too close. So it is often with Christians receiving the Holy Spirit. Things not of God which are hidden within them surface and begin to manifest themselves in blatant ways.

An old friend, Brother Rufus Moseley, once commented on this very phenomenon: "A bush may have rattlesnakes hidden around its base, yet it appears lovely and harmless because no one knows the snakes are there. But set that bush on fire and see what happens to the snakes! They come forth writhing and hissing!" Some Christians never discover they need deliverance from evil spirits until after they receive the baptism in the Holy Spirit.

3) Satan will try to convince you that impressions from him are really from God.

We've already pointed out that both God and Satan are active in the supernatural realm. Unfortunately, many newly charismatic Christians ignore this truth and fall into the trap of accepting every spiritual impulse as coming directly from the Holy Spirit. They insist they are being "led by the spirit." Maybe so, but the question is, *what* spirit?

Remember how Jesus, when He was confronted by the devil in the wilderness, answered each temptation with Scripture? The only safe way to check the myriad of spiritual impressions which begin coming our way after receiving the Holy Spirit is by carefully checking and comparing them with the written Word of God. We dare not rely on subjective feelings alone; they are much too unreliable. No matter how spiritual we may feel about some leading, or how strongly we may be prompted to accept some strange new revelation, if it is contrary to the Word of God, it is not from the Holy Spirit. *The Spirit of God and the Word of God always agree.*

I know some Spirit-baptized Christians who became so enamored of the "new" revelations and prophecies they were receiving that they broke fellowship with more stable friends who insisted on checking the revelation by Scripture. They accused their friends of "quenching the Spirit." Among the new revelations was one which claimed that one of the pregnant young women in their group was to give birth to the "new Messiah," and that this event was to be the second coming of Christ.

On another occasion, a young minister caught up in his own subjective experiences boasted to me, "I don't need the Bible any more. I'm receiving my revelations directly from God Himself!"

Make no mistake about it: *all spiritual revelations and all subjective spiritual experiences need to be confirmed by the Word of God.* Any experience contrary to the teaching or the spirit of Scripture should be quickly discarded, no matter how exciting it sounds or how plausible it appears. If it does not conform to Scripture, it is either the result of an overactive spiritual imagination, or it is a deception from the father of lies himself.

"Beloved, do not believe every spirit, but test the spirits to see whether they are of God; for many false prophets have gone out into the world" (1 John 4:1).

My prayer is that the Holy Spirit would keep you out of deception and lead you into the complete truth of our Lord Jesus Christ.

Supplement to the Revised Edition

We trust these added words of instruction and counsel given in Chapter 6 will in no way hinder or discourage those seeking to release the spiritual potential of the baptism in the Holy Spirit. They have been added to the original text for two reasons. First, to help the many who become unduly dismayed over the reaction of friends and family to their new experience; and second, to offer practical advice concerning the spiritual warfare which we all find ourselves in, once we enter the supernatural realm of the Spirit.

—Don W. Basham

Other titles from Kidwell Publishing available through your favorite bookstore or online at: www.kidwellpublishing.com

The Pilgrim's Progress – Part I and Part II
By John Bunyan
ISBN: 978-0-9817634-3-9

This timeless class of John Bunyan "delivered under the similtude of a dream" captures the hearts and minds of readers with Bunyan's depth of understanding and scriptural knowledge, as well as his subtle comedy and witticisms. This edition contains both parts of Bunyan's tale, including all of the original scripture references in an easy-to-read format.

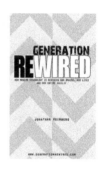

Generation Rewired
By Jonathan Heimberg
ISBN: 978-0-9817634-2-2

Generation Rewired is an informative look into the world of technology, and how it is subtly changing the way we work, live and think. Examining the social networking phenomenon and other pervasive technologies, this book is an eye-opening, quick read that will thoroughly change the way you view technology.

Freedom To Choose
By E. L. Kidwell
ISBN: 978-0-9817634-1-5

Visit the Kingdom of Heaven before Earth was created. Enter the throne room of God, and experience the events before time began. Discover the secrets of why hell's chief accuser betrayed the love and perfection of His Creator, and set himself to destroy the race of mankind in seething hatred. Enjoy this thought-provoking drama as it brings to life the Genesis account of the Bible, probes the spiritual aspects of humanity, and amplifies the brilliance of the scriptures.

(continued)

Offering Stories, Quotes, and Illustrations
By Robert Polaco
ISBN: 978-0-9817634-5-3
This book is a compilation of over 200 offering stories, quotes, and illustrations. Each illustration also contains a note line where pastors or administrators can indicate the date on which the illustration was used, preventing the potential embarrassment of reusing an illustration. This is a must have companion for any pastor or church administrator.

The Labyrinth of Shadow
By Aly Lyn
ISBN: 978-0-9817634-4-6
Peace was predicted in the ancient writings, and a rising power claimed lordship of all the lands. After seven years of tranquility, the people have been lulled into a false state of security. Forgotten in the ancient writings was the warning of what else would come. Enter the Labyrinth of Shadow, an exciting world of fantastic creatures, and action-packed adventure!

Christian Living:
Encouragement for Growing Christians
By E. L. Kidwell
ISBN: 978-0-9817634-0-8
Like the body, the soul needs a healthy diet to grow. And an essential nutrient for spiritual growth is encouragement! This book contains a collection of messages on relevant issues to help every growing Christian be all they can be in Christ. This book is categorized topically for use as a Bible study guide, devotional help, or for spiritual reference.

CPSIA information can be obtained
at www.ICGtesting.com
Printed in the USA
BVHW070620230622
640383BV00002B/380